⎼⎼ⱮⱮⱮⱮⱮ⎼⎼ Coloratura On A Silence
Found In Many Expressive Systems

ALSO BY ALICE FULTON

Poetry

Barely Composed

Cascade Experiment: Selected Poems

Felt

Sensual Math

Powers Of Congress

Palladium

Dance Script With Electric Ballerina

Fiction

The Nightingales of Troy: Connected Stories

Essays

Feeling as a Foreign Language: The Good Strangeness of Poetry

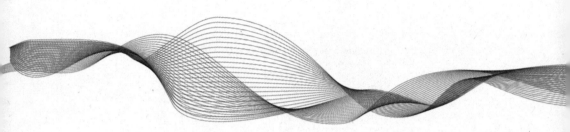

W. W. NORTON & COMPANY
Independent Publishers Since 1923

Coloratura On A Silence
Found In Many Expressive Systems

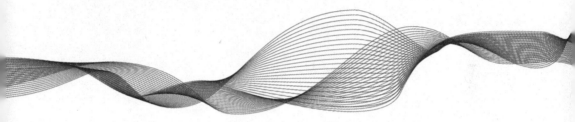

POEMS

Alice Fulton

For information about permission to reproduce selections from this book, write to
Permissions, W. W. Norton & Company, Inc., 500 Fifth Avenue, New York, NY 10110

For information about special discounts for bulk purchases, please contact
W. W. Norton Special Sales at specialsales@wwnorton.com or 800-233-4830

Manufacturing by Versa Press
Production manager: Julia Druskin

ISBN: 978-1-324-02108-7

W. W. Norton & Company, Inc., 500 Fifth Avenue, New York, N.Y. 10110
www.wwnorton.com

W. W. Norton & Company Ltd., 15 Carlisle Street, London W1D 3BS

1 2 3 4 5 6 7 8 9 0

For Hank

and remembering my parents,
Jack and Mary

Contents

Four

Five

Six

‑‑ⅧⅧⅧ‑‑ **Coloratura On A Silence**

Found In Many Expressive Systems

At The Feast

I stand in line to be inoculated against time. Will you join me?
While night goes by like a cortege, and the stars are busy
being charming. Being heaven's trinkets. Gleamers, why so brightly?
You occupy the trauma darkness yet seem robotic, all numbed up.
When were you appointed to bear witness? And by whom?
You are not special, accidentals. You're too many,
and what kindness comes when heaven's overwhelmed?
Witness is too big a word. Testimony's full of moan, so I'll say it
in sidereal. Tell it to the stars. Little spitfires, poached in gilt,
I'll empathize. Say you are not glittering but flinching.
Distant listeners maybe do the same for me: say shivering
is shine when that's all I have to give. At the feast,
steak knives tapped the crystal flutes to sound your music,
heaven's gristle, tiny chimes that you alone make visible.

One

Netherlandish

To witness constant miracle is a distraction.
In its presence, I wore earbuds, snowflake sleepers—
a design of teensy pounce wheels, no two unalike.

      An eraser workshop, snow fell
on the boreal forest, my thoughts
dark firs. The palette was dingy: dishwater
grays, sweat yellows—the colors of
the pillow stuffed with balsam

      needles we used as a doorstop
while the plow foundered in the yard,
the storm door balked on orogenies of snow.

I was living in a high-maintenance loneliness,
researching the mean winter temperature,

      water weirded into nonce ideals,
forms whose bowels were struts of ice,

      the crystal's airy crotch.
Things that evolved to house the marvelous
for which there is no counterfeit.
Like the sun appearing like

      the orange in a Christmas stocking's toe.

You have to make love to the corners,

      my mother quoted her mother

as she scrubbed the sepia tape stains
where the poster was torn down.
     The Adoration of the Magi in the Snow,
a scene of labor more than adoration
though there must be a likeness between
sublime laws and those who toil under them.

Only kings can afford such worship.
If the workers paused to marvel
their chores would go undone.
     They'd hammer their thumbs.
They were thinking about leverage. Lunch.
     If summer comes, I'll change to paisley
sleepers, a childish word. There will be cornucopias
all over me—pink, orange, green—a host of
     horns of plenty. This snow

has been falling for ages.
It has turned into firn, the word for ancient snow.
Something is emerging, crudely rendered
     in the nethermost
left of the painting—rags in frass,
     larval squirm, a maggot
immanence, the size of a cursor.
I've tried to see it on these screens

everyone keeps touching
        tenderly as lovers. On my tiny device,

I can't make it out. Whatever
        is taking shape took shape
without any procreation.
Yet everything it touches becomes
an erogenous zone. That's how you know
        you're in the presence of a god.
If you're looking for the marvelous,
look to the margins.
        If you're looking for a miracle,
look to the invisible.

Coloratura On A Darkness Chosen From A Gamut Of Stygian Events

As I was saying, winter was my season, night my time
in that room like the plush-lined case
where a wind instrument lives.
I was petrified, nothing much
was expected of me, bound in
corsets, stabilizers, unable to do much
more than speak. The luxury, the horror.
The days of grace were over,
the complacency I possessed
as a young woman walking
into a diner with an acquaintance,
an engineer, a techie, from the radio station
where I'd worked—Al, who'd suffered
a catastrophic accident
and could only utter muddy sentences
dragged from the guts of cognition.
It was a tongue spoken in a country of one.
I might have mentioned Frida Kahlo,
The Broken Column, as he painstakingly ate
and in his fractured voice explained
his plan to be a velvet painter.
Later that century, when I taught night
classes, a student called his poems "procedures,"
relishing the word's glint of anesthesia, frigid instruments,

and later still I was on something
called the Procedure Committee,
a title I wanted changed

to Happiness Consortium. Euphemism
has its uses. Al called his seizures "episodes,"
as if they told stories, while I turned the pages
of the boothside jukebox, fed it
coins to fill the air with a sprightly vocal
and crystalline piccolo trumpet—sunny, nostalgic—
"Penny Lane," an old song even then.
When I looked at Al I saw him flickering
between what he was now and how
he'd been at the station tending
to a wall of tiny blinking bulbs. Claustrophilia
began in the control room,
with its cauterized electronic
smell, its hint of vinyl, dustmites, meters
with mini windshield wipers.
It was where one turned into many,
into words. You needed an air voice like ice wine
for classical, whiskey for jazz. Coke for rock.
The red light warned we were live
as my voice seeped through the foam
windscreen, the mic's starfield perforations,
to enter unknown bodies via the ear, traveling

its darkly narrow corridor to the drum
that conveyed vibrations to a trinity of tiny
bones, amplifying the sound
and sending it to the deepest reaches of the inner
part shaped like a mollusk,
where fluid rippled and cells surfed

                      the sonic
wave till it opened at last in a chemical rush of electric
impulses carried by a nerve to the brain,
which heard my voice.
Listening is a country of one.
Callers wanted Satin Doll and got Sun Ra.
At midnight, I signed off classical
with *Eine kleine Nachtmusik*
and began the all-night jazz show.
As the voice teachers say, you have to listen louder
than you sing. When Al first phoned I'd laughed
at his distorted voice. It had been years,
I'd moved on and hadn't heard
about his injury. He'd always been a kidder.
I thought he was trying some new schtick.
We'd never been on the same wavelength,
you see. Empathy invites contagion, you feel
permeated, a proxy for the trauma at large.
But what I feel this minute is fear
of pimping off another's pain. Is anybody there?

Narcissus called, and Echo said there, there.
Come to me, he called. And she replied me, me.
No matter what you write you write yourself
as I wrote in my sickroom while snow fell
and wind sounded like the bristly velcro
of my leg stabilizer ripping. It was striped
and almost sporty. The black wrist corset looked

                                        fetishistic

with its laces. If you must have materiality,
it's best to be a crystal, anomalous and silent.
I could see winter through two windows.
Falling snow framed shapes of negative space.
We see what we say. I wrote by talking
to my phone and night,
my only visitor, always came on time.
I learned white flowers—tuberose, gardenia, jasmine—
do their best work after dark.
There was no evidence of effort as cut and stuck
in vases they exhaled their complex scents.
The stargazer lilies smelled like Chanel—
like the beginning of the last
century, when perfumes were first
carbonated by aldehydes unfolding in accords,
a fragrance unlike any found in nature so I've heard.
Everything—even products sold as unscented—even cold
has an odor, even snow—there is—isn't

there——a breath of ozone when it falls,
a freshness you bring in after being out

in it, a smell trapped in
the folds of your clothes. Ice wine,
pressed from grapes frozen on the vine,
requires the bitter winters of the Finger Lakes,
months of crystals needling its pulp
to produce a cloying nose of apricot and honey.
Certain odors lodge in the esophagus
and you can't stop smelling them long after.
Who was Al's caregiver, I wondered, who helped him
when he painted, tightening his grip, letting quivering
inflect his singular style. Who listened
as he described his process—how he was inspired
by the Flemish Golden Age, by Manet,
how velvet was absorbent and he liked that
when he started the black areas
were already done. I wondered what
therapist prescribed this effort-
ful labor, what psycho-
analyst advised that trauma
could be calmed by globs of bright acrylic on dark.
Who said bone grows back, imagine
tiny needles knitting, though there are limits—
that must be admitted. There, there.

12

In the diner, Al showed me one of his velvet
paintings, a black fur flaunting fleshy
roses, groins of petals, vines inspired
by an ivy tendril growing through

his windowsill, creeping like a bass line
of plutonic rock, and I stared and marveled
as he shakily ate his soup. As my gaze wavered
between iridescent white, seething magenta, tactile
black, I might have glimpsed chimerical colors
that can't be seen with ordinary vision, impossible
shades outside the spectrum, uncharted
hues with no materiality that only appear
when the eyes' cone cells are exhausted.
A student introduced me to these
hybrids you have to cross
your eyes to see, unfocusing, following procedures.
Stygian blue, my favorite, was an ocean coma
of saturated navy-black, self-luminous
red glowed even on paper, which doesn't
emit light, hyperbolic orange exceeded
one hundred percent density to be more
orange than any orange
in the gamut. In experiments,
observers couldn't name these spectral
colors though some perceived them

for a while afterward. Of course,
my meeting with Al took place years before
I started teaching and was taught
such mongrel facts. In the diner, I'd been embarrassed
by his crass blacklight botanicals,
which to be completely naked with you now
hold aesthetic possibilities for me—
                                        being low
on the commodity scale, déclassé, attractive
to those who follow their passions
and repulsive to those with what's called taste—
those who prefer artisanal over kraft velveeta, say.
O you shunn'd paintings! I will be your poet.
Hah! In truth, I also like artisanal.
There's a trend called dark table dining,
restaurants named Opaque, Dans le Noir,
which are spaces utterly devoid of light.
No luminous watches, no shining
devices allowed. The interior is pitch. Prepare
for adventure, the ad says. Prepare
for a bold dive into otherness, an experience
that enhances gustatory nuances, educates
the sighted and empowers the blind.
I think I got that right. You have to sign
a legal waiver before going through
the light-lock. A visually impaired server

guides you, explains where the cutlery is placed.
Your eyes do not adjust. Still, your mind paints
images wherever your gaze falls. The space
is clattering, suffocating. You sample
a perfumey paste and wind up
eating with your hands. It is solitary.
A person loses all spatial orientation.
A person turns to voice. Is anybody

                          there?

Some panic and have to be escorted out.
Dessert is black forest cake.
White canes are handed out as souvenirs.
No, that's a joke the server told.
For me this touristy attempt at empathy,
trying blindness for a spell, an interval
with a sighted ending, falls so far
short it's sinister. This way
we must meet. But who am I
to say. Once upon a life I used my father's cellar shop
as a makeshift darkroom. The warped door
locked only from the outside, so
my mother had to lift it slightly, push, and swivel
a tiny wooden latch from vertical to horizontal
over the crack to excise all light and shut me in
that nox extreme where I'd shake
cans of film at a utility sink. Developer,

acid, fixative. I tried not to think
about being buried alive, a fear
of my father's, and when I finished,

I'd call my mother to release me.
My father was dead, did I mention,
which changes everything.
For some, there is no end to dark.
A friend used to accompany a blind singer
whose bass voice sounded the depths
like a surgeon inferring how deep his chisel
reaches by a change in sound
when the instrument goes through bone
into a hole. As this singer's voice fell
you felt you heard
the drop in the gallows, the way down
swift followed by a swift
finality. Come to me. The gorges here
are frightening, a feature of the sublime.
One night following a formal dinner
thinking all her guests had left, the host
snuffed the outside lights, leaving me
to walk a narrow ascent between
two steep drops, alone
but for my mobile, which for some reason—
but wait, heads up, the red light's on. Who's listening

to my all-night gig? It was my job
to tame the dark, accompany hundreds
—or a handful— through it.
The classical station's control room
was housed in a TV studio vast as a cathedral,

but darker, without candles. Serpents
of thick cords stretched or coiled across the floor.
You could fall. The ceiling was invisible.
If suddenly illuminated I fancied I'd be dazzled
by an elaborate mural painted by someone
on a high and trembling scaffold, a fresco
that started to dissolve the instant it saw light.
Al had a friend, an outsider artist before the term
existed, who made disturbing snowglobes.
Where you'd expect a plaid log cabin
or sleigh with smiling reindeer,
there'd be panicked horses trapped
in a burning van, a human
being garroted. Choke. Strangles.
Wobbles. Founder. Slobbers. Heaves. Shivers.
Equine suffering delves into the farthest viscera
of English. I shut my eyes and am permeated
by strains of ancient
music on internet fm as I click away, computing
the hours of daylight that remain.

In the dead of night during my convalescence,
I sometimes was awoken
by a boreal aroma so palpable it seemed
to hang in air, a globe or gibbous
fragrance of the forest floor
that lasted only seconds before ceasing
abruptly as a light switch clicking off,
which made me think it was a

                      phantom
scent, an olfactory chimera.
I was laid out, did I say, in the bedroom
where my mother died, a cavity of anguish.
For some, there is no end to night.
In her last years, she'd lost her sense
of smell, which dulled her
sense of taste. Is anybody there? During the day
I'd watch miracle people on TV
going about their casual errands,
parking lot to big box store, and envy
the weightshift that was walking, a primal dance
they took for granted as I had before
fractures turned me to a voice-
writer—each word a coloratura
that vanished the instant it existed,
which wasn't, as I've said, a first.
Before the radio gigs I'd been an information operator

repeating five words eight hours a day
with two fifteen-minute breaks.
Directory Assistance, for what city? In Edinburgh
as a tourist, I stayed out late alone,
so the b & b had been put to sleep
when I returned. The hallways, lacking nightlights,
were stygian rivers. I think I used math
to make my way, counting doorknobs,
stroking the walls, taking a chance at last

                         at what

might be the right room. This way we will meet.
The brain is a magician, but there are limits—
that must be admitted. There
was a game I liked as a tiny child. My big sisters
would schlep me in a blanket
to a place of their choosing and abandon me. The fun
was in not knowing where I'd be
when I emerged. They promised not to leave
me in some scary crypt, but kids themselves,
adolescents, they found my terror hilarious
and couldn't resist the chance
to stow me under the dark
dining room table or inside a crushing closet.
Give me a voice stabilizer, please ==
a spirit that calls in.
When I was young enough to still be living

with my mother, she pounded on my bedroom door,
alarmed, yelling Al, come out!
The warped door of my father's cellar shop
had somehow locked, the door

that required muscle—a lift, a shove—
before the tiny latch would turn
and hold it closed. We went down to find
there'd been no break, no entering, there
was no one there. Somehow
the door had locked itself.
My mother wouldn't believe in ghosts
even if she saw one. It's a common fear,
the eye doctor said, when I told him
how the night before I'd opened my eyes
and was unable to discern a thing,
blind for what seemed too long
a time. Twice now I've passed
some ticking meridian—fallen
unconscious, gone
into anon, a party of none, decoupled suddenly
from time, and I can testify
that when it comes
to darkness there is no comparison.
What's your name, who's this,
what day is it? It wasn't losing it,

wasn't the concussed headache
and retching afterward that terrorized,
it was that I'd returned from nonexistence knowing
there was a where where there
was no night no dark no
time. When I tried to explain it there was no

way. I write to write it
out, the frightful cold. Science,
which is always
changing and explaining,
at this writing says reality
can mend itself. It's been proven
by a bit sent into the past
that had no effect upon the present.
A complex spectrum of
connectedness, a gamut of
entanglement that can be
influenced with a breath, I still believe
the large comes from the small
nonlinear effects, tiny triggers,
"a sensitive dependence on
initial conditions," which at this
writing might be mystical
more than scientific. I make no claims.
An atheist at three a.m., I pray for God

because nothing is all powerful,
pray whatever helps
this feverish planet be
comforted itself,
and every morsel
comprising us be
healed == while the concept == just
the concept == of
a paraclete yields brightness ==
please == to me.

Two

Chrome Yellow With A Rose

Silent as chakras
        they circumambulated
their cloudy bowl
        that had no basking light,
just a mermaid
        lounging on a bridge
like a louche chanteuse on a piano.
        They were red-eared sliders
but to me, as a child,
        they were just turtles
retracting into shells.
        One had a painted carapace—
chrome yellow with a rose.
        They weren't ornaments,
yet they keep slipping into metaphor
        as if they existed to
stand for something else, their fate
        through the ages. As everyone knows
                the earth rests on a turtle
                        that rests on a turtle
                                and it's turtles all the way
down, an infinite regress.
"You're a Professor Decrepita
        and you don't know

how to take selfies?"
        She shamed me
but I would not be ashamed.
        Find out what it means
to me as the Queen
        sang. I knew a few things.
I knew I lived
        in young mountains
that started massive years ago.
        Orogeny happens
when things converge.
        If you're deep into self-
interest, assuming the earth
        rests on you alone, well,
it's narcissism all the way down.
        I knew I was present
                for a blip of forever
                        but for a long time
                                I didn't know the word
for the color of my eyes.
Heterochromatic. Blue spruce
        with an amber circle.
Only one came close
        enough to notice.
I knew the end of civil twilight
        looked like the beginning

26

of civil dawn. Great things happened
       and I thought they were the start
of a florious process
       that would lead to major
floribunda
       when in fact they were
the florabundance.
       If I'd seen the future
I'd have died of grief
       in the womb. Let's not
and say we did.
       It's not supposed to be easy, this.
          There's winter
              with its live-edge wind.
                  The campus on the hill
that gave me mountain sickness.
Big ice. Big squeeze. Scree.
       I conversed with God
who had questions
       re: life on earth. You're asking me,
a nonbeliever? Do I have any credence?
       When you're indelible,
the force that sparks the thermal burst
       that tells the body it's alive. God,
I just heard two people speaking
       the world's most beautiful language.

I think the French invented it
        just to impress people,
which is how most people think
        of poetry. They were discussing
ulterior motives, the subterfuge
        that underscored this tragic year,
though I might have misheard
        "time's electric spurs."
                My knowledge couldn't help
                        my raisons d'être
                                who were innocence
all the way down. Infinite regrets.
"If you want to come back
        you will," God said.
"But you have to be willing
        to come back
as something else. Software
        for a floating wind farm. Tarmac.
And you have to bring your tears."
        There's that. I brought my tears
when I came back.
        They entered the aquifer.
Things prograde toward water
        in geology while in astronomy
to prograde is to spin. To be alive
        is to be ordained ==

the wondering consort
        of so much world. Poetry is full of it.
So much beauty, so much
        world. I don't know
                what to do with it, do you?
                        You can == you can't
                                quite rinse the joy from it.
You can study with adepts. Scientists
who conduct thought experiments.
        Poets who say which is to say. Intensivists
who'll blow on your chakras
        to bring you back. Red-eared sliders
can live a hundred years
        in the wild. Mine lived maybe a few months.
Recipient Unknown,
        when I'm postheart,
will you breathe
        on my chakras by reading this?
This writing might who knows
        slip or spin through time
to you. Emotions like this
        should be painted
with a single-hair brush.
        You can spit on it
to hone the point. See here

I left a shell, a strand.
　　See here she left
　　　　a strand, a shell.

Cauterized Keepsake Gift Boxes

She decided to write her posthumous poems while she was still alive. The problem was they were dead simple and had only two lines. White space can do wonders, the Coachman said. Consider a cutaway diagram, lookbook, and pink bow at the end. But her ribbons were pinked not pink, her bows freestanding and said to have a menacing presence. Their pointed parts suggested incisors, stingers, talons.

She was curled up cozily on the edge of a gorge. She could smell the waterfall boiling over mixed with the scent of writers sweating their shapes onto the page and artists drawing blood. It would not hold still. Her old friends had all gone together to pluck wild mountain thyme. One who was a candle's surrogate had given her a cauterized keepsake before leaving. Maps no longer answered to her location. After her phone fell through the fretwork of the bridge's suicide net, the Coachman said you're good to go. He was speaking to light and time. To her, he said hurry, the daylilies close at 8:45.

She was trying to trace the subtle butterfly effect that cascaded to her downfall. Mobbed, shadow banned. Never invited to their "at homes." Scorn clouds gathered. Was it because she'd said women who weren't feminists were victims of the Stockholm syndrome, bonding with misogyny to survive? After his tongue was cut out by the maenads, he had it replaced with his penis, which explains everything, the apologists said. She thought it was a stretch. There was

31

much she didn't understand. Pie charts without pies, caffeine-free javascript. The polarized folk on the Commons searching for commonality when being alive ticked all the boxes.

She needed an intentional community and friendly weeping space. Trees weep, wounds weep, literary diction weeps. But humans cry, the Coachman said, and asked her to envision his latest rough mix. It would not hold still, so she decided to accompany it. She was tuning her air guitar and wondering whether the satisfaction of carving out time would be worth the bother of searching for a butcher knife when she smelled the taxidermy of a bow. It was a noxious odor. A candle can do only so much. She wondered what its flame looked like after it had been blown out. I'll always love you even when it seems I don't. I'll always be with you even when it seems I'm not. Those were the two lines.

Elliptical Furnace

The diamond inhaled light
        and exhaled fire. It boasted
a brilliant cut anatomy

        and a language. This one
gets the booby prize,
        my mother declared, and I laughed

and cried as her words blew
        through me and asked her
to inscribe them on my latest.

        Her pink refrigerator threatened
to cave under the weight of
        paper shingled to its door.

The card from her friend
        Esther that arrived after Esther
died. My thank-you letter

        from Yoko with "I agree"
scribbled by John as postscript
        had been lost. Throw that one in

the elliptical furnace.
        The diamond was taken
into back rooms, kept

        overnight and removed
from its setting to be appraised.
        Pavilion. Crown. Table.

I'd laminated the letter
        to preserve it which destroyed
its market value. The fabled sound

        sculpture was made of pipes
with holes the wind sang through.
        He rested his head

on its base to augment
        the aural dimension
with bone conduction scintillations

        and licked it for sublingual
absorption. I offered
        the sheet music. It was Chopin's

Étude in A-flat Major,
        "Aeolian Harp,"
but he couldn't read it.

        Diamonds exist to blurb
the third finger of the left.
        I didn't want the setting

and planned to have it
        melted down. I didn't
want the crying

        and planned to make it breathing—
try some semantic bleaching—
        when I revised.

Motherese

If she had to be in it, she'd want it to be happy,
without many dictionary words
like the language mothers speak
to their children, a tongue too heart-driven
to be taught. The experts at the spiritual home
of Speech Act Theory called it Motherese,
"an illocutionary force"
and "acme of ordinariness."
My sister who's a mother spoke it
to our mother when she was dying.
We never said certain dire words
since she'd forget and ask again,
again. We came up with lying
niceties, told a varnished truth.
   Will I get better?
There was hope, the thing with talons,
in her tone and trust.
The experts said "one fulfills sincerity
conditions by precisely indicating
the genuineness of a request."
   Where are the real nurses?
When she was afraid
her first day in kindergarten, her mother
walked back and forth outside the window.

And night upon night
as she died she called
  Mother
her summons steadfast, soft,
till an exasperated doomgiver
said Mary, your mother's dead. She's been dead
for sixty years. And Ma didn't realize
she was crying as tears ran down her cheeks
and the nightgiver changed the station
to coma drones == music trying to pass
for music creeping through the morphine cracks.
  This is my fault, isn't it.
The experts were full of if and only if.
The nightgiver cited God. I could not
experience the depth of this
dropeverything witness I was living ==
couldn't think dropeverything through ==
  I'm dying, aren't I?
Sincerity? Conditions? Precisely?
Indicate? An illocutionary force
was needed == to blow the whole
thing up == she was == being
forcibly touched == by an abyss ==
how far from == happy == I was == enabling
an impossibility == I could not
experience == feelings stoked by

== her clothes were all that held her ==
== my clothes were all that held me ==
       Read to me.
Her last request. But I could not
think dropeverything what. The experts said
each word constitutes its own problem
space. Like a piano with a missing string
there's a hole once dropeverything is over.
There's this memory
fugue that brings me to my grief.
A bird can wield its boney tongue
and double-throated syrinx to sound
two notes at once, dueting
with itself and in a way ==
       that's what I've done.

Salt Point Vesper

I feel the manacle inside my wrist, screws and plate inside my leg
as we ramble through Salt Point, this bird sanctuary with an industrial past.
"All the steam in the world could not, like the Virgin, build Chartres."

Long ago, a little church stood here, built by Syrian immigrants
who harvested salt. When the plant closed, it became a site for dumping,
drugs. Friends of Salt Point changed it to a haven. I've learned

the tibial plateau is not a place. Everything rests on it. I tell myself
I'm doing great since my mother isn't here to say it. God help us,
she might say if she could see my state. It was simple.

Rescuing horses led to this. Broken. Kicked. Who wants lame
mules, slow Thoroughbreds? I met the meatman's deadlines, paid
to keep them from his truck, the panicked trek to Canada

and captive bolt. The little free library is crammed with castoffs,
humidity wraps me like a damp pashmina. Schvitzy. Like omniscience.
The sun is shining in its fickle way, and though I limp, I live

to witness its fair minutes. What would you like to wear? my sister asked
my mother on her deathbed. *A dress.* Not a shroud of repurposed catalytic
converter stuff. God knows not a body bag. Is there an Upholder

of the tranquil soul? The Office of Spirituality and Meaning Making
maintains a website. Is the force of love too fierce? I'm asking.
All the salt in the world could not, like our questions, build tears.

Ampersand Inscriptions

My sister told me waving tree branches caused the wind
       & as a child I believed they did.
She was sure God existed & I thought maybe
       she could believe for me
this sister so sure while I was thinking

       God's been going on as long as luck
which was what I had for God.
       I saw her on google maps watering some lacey thing
redbud == acacia == two shrubs with pink blossoms
       a terracotta planter like the one she gave me,

the lawn thirsty & sky bright as it always is
       where she is   if you try you might see
your sister too though when I looked again
       black door == black shutters == blinds drawn
& I admit she never told me

       that thing about the trees & wind—
though believing in God seems almost
       similar? I'm thinking maybe
the shamers, haters, need my sister
       to love for them—what

a paraclete would do
        if such a thing existed   as it does in her
old books I discovered in the attic as a kid—
        a red hair in *Wuthering Heights* & at the end
body could not keep up with the spirit written in her hand

Three

A Thing Long Thought And Kind

A gift is a risk. Let roses be the prodrome.
It's like it dropped a gold and a silver

ring with its name on it
in my brain. That was the gift

before the storm. It sent you a stumbling
block. Just scribble yes or no

on the form. Now every time the doorbell
rings I think someone's sent me one.

A gift is a guess. Did it come close?
It's what you need most

that turns you nerve side out. Right
now I think I'm growing something

long thought and kind of
clumsy. Just wrap it in drafts with awk

in the margins. Stuff it
in a wooden pillow with a drawer.

A gift is a task. It could be mustard
or rust. You have to decide

whether to send those flowers that drop
whole from the stem or

the ones whose petals fall one
by one. You know how rain will

turn the roses nerve side out?
A gift is a test. They need to know that.

When she wrote their thorns
are the best part of them I can't begin

to tell you how many kinds of
right she was. Now I think I'm growing

something long thought
to be the prerogative of certain

entitled individuals. Wings
or barbs. When all I wanted was

a more subtle pulse
at the throat bone. Well, what size

do you wear? I am smelting you a surprise.
Not another luminous lyre

cum lint remover. Take it
from me. If you depend on gifts

for what you need you'll end up with
a gold and a silver shoe

both for the same lame foot.

Bracelet With Dictatorial Erotics

He was toying with her charms,
fascinated she thought by otherness.
        Though it might have been the elfin intricacy
of gizmos preceding bytes and bits, before

digital technology, the lure of
        lilliputian replicas, a hurdy-gurdy
with a churning handle—I like her
premise better: he was taken

by his first glimpse of a fetching feminine
        realm and her sterling charms
were the code he'd break or calibrate.
Maybe he was hoping for a dainty V8

engine combusting on essential oils,
a shrunken bucking bronco. Boy stuff.
        Maybe he thought he was discovering
a new facet of electromagnetism. Lust.

The girl pretended not to notice him
fingering her finery. She didn't want to make him
        take up arms. She was sporting
boyish brogues, a gift from her dad,

wearing them to spare his feelings,
        though the brown cladding was ugly as dung
beetles, overgrown warts
saddening her feet. She was riding

        a three-speed she called Bullet.
It was almost summer. Soon
        they'd be tortured by hormones, rampant
humidity, soaring pollen counts.

Tangled enchantments, puzzle crushes.
        Rage. They'd shake like shadows.
Pass them the antidote. Send harvest wind.
        Till someday in this living

        she'll still have the bracelet—
and quivering from a distance
        when the play of light allows—
its tiny shackled star.

Beauty School

Dad said if I didn't graduate from high school
he'd buy me my own beauty shop. And that's pretty
much how it went. I worked on heads.
      My students gave me wise advice.
One said the best critique came from a friend
who just wrote Wonderful! Keep going!
on every poem. Another said his favorite mentor
      simply put a giant X on any page he didn't like.
Some had studied with lyric pooh-bahs
who taught them to be coffee wallahs.

Do birds theorize flying? I believe the best poetry
      instruction leans toward the oblique.

"This seems to be a ransacked candle.
This tastes like Iowa. This reads
like the shortest building in the world
      trying to be tall. This syntax feels kissed.
This is like a bandage
that takes the skin off with it.
These lines look laser-cut;
      these need to be debrided, flayed.
Forget Esperanto. This is written
in Blackwatch Plaid. Did you use a protractor

or a pen to compose it? That school
        of poetics is called ellipsograph tech.

Lyric poets give their words to the wind.
It's how the wind stays alive. To riff
on Miles Davis, you don't have to write
        your poem every day.
You just have to touch your poem
every day. Even if it sounds like mucus
made for the glory of God
        or twinkles like a pissed-off
harpsichord. Even if it groans like a medieval
cathedral, eroded at the groins. You've heard

how flaws authenticate a gem? Usher in a stir
        and weird the real. Forget the celestial

and remember the celeste—
an organ stop that's tuned to dissonance
to torque the note. Tone
        is the soul of poetry.
If you need a title 'Lonely Consort
Of Wandering Phenomenon' works
for almost anything. When revising think
        how a robin throwing himself against the glass
won't change it into air."
Poetry is never finished.

Only poets are. Some must be
     wrapped in burlap to survive.

Some must flash their stitches = =
though the deepest scars
are hidden, the damaged infra-
     trauma they intend to tell.
One bent her lines backwards
like the ankles of a sandhill crane.
One unzipped his surface to reveal
     his furtive fretwork. They all held their breaths
until their tongues turned blue.
Wonderful! Keep going!

One Toe Pointing Backwards Prodrome

This feeling—that you could have grown wings.
You could be so flying. Many did this,
though it took a zillion years.
Start with attached flaps that spread
against the air to give a lifting force.
Your first glides will be short and steep.
You'll need nostrils on top of your head,

and brains no bigger than a hen's eggs.
There's always a price. Any bones not used
for gliding will be lost. You'll have to specialize.
You'll have to live in forests made of rotting
swamps, clubmosses, liverworts. You'll have to grow
horns and crests, bony shields around your neck,
a helmet with air tubes, webbed appendages, hooves.

All flying comes at a cost. You'll have to have dirty hair,
be duck-billed, thick-skulled,
enfluffled with fuzzage.
Your first wings will have claws and one toe
pointing backwards. You'll be horned-faced,
beak-snouted. You'll have open sores
from fighting and putrid flesh

between your teeth. You'll have to stink.
Your stomachs will move into your feets.
You'll shrink. Your wings will be long
as a jet's, your body the size of a turkey vulture.
Your skin will turn to scales
before it turns to plumage.
You'll have to sleep upside down or kneeling.

You'll be tempted to give up, say fuck it,
when you could have raised a sail
on your back to collect the sun.
You could have thought
of those who'd come after,
how you might endow them.
When things evolve they cast their shadows.

It's a sweet reveal.
Or shall a twig or any floating thing
. . . point me out my course?
Evolution has no idea
where it's going till it gets there.
You'll have to croak like a crocodile.
You'll have to honk for umpteen years

before you sing. And while you're trying
to be the lyre whose only compass is the wind,

you won't have forever. You'll always feel
the spinning fuselage of overness
that falls on everything. And what comes after
having come so far? You'll have to be
a starling rather than a star.

Blue Funk Stew Dialogic

The gift consisted of erasers and a tiny comb with missing teeth.
Objects have agency. I didn't know what to make of it.

       Would you rather be an ornament or a tool?
The box contained a procedural guide with *precisely* in every skill
set and many ways of spelling marginal.
O you shunn'd persons! Mobbed. Othered. It's coin of the realm.

       Why did you want to come here?

       No one knows you and you won't have any friends.
They curate & cancel, preen & huzzah.
Don't rain on their charade. Don't dampen their harangue.
Introduce polarizing film to soften the glare. Say I see
and be their neverbeing. Think not
of structures larded with main-sequence stars. Think not
of pompous bureaucrats born to be parade marshals.
Harrumph, harrumph. Say *wonderful* caressingly
and praise those who smell triumphant,
though your tongue is disgusted by the taste
of your mouth, its only house.

       What is the sauce of their crypto-colonialism?
Smiling won't hide it. The question boils
down to devouring ghosts.
Like a prisoner I stood before locked doors
waiting for them to open. I come forthwith in your midst—

       You will be our interlocutor, facilitator.

Our bespoke cohort defines you.
A locked door emits energy. Dejection,
like a detested music, can never be turned low enough.

 No worries. Tonedeaf tech will find a way.
No, this pukesome music will never be minimally invasive.
It will never be quiet enough. Some tunes, like coigns,
have weaponized projecting corners.

 Do hearts?
Discouragement is low maintenance. I feel mine bounce
against my bones. There are many ways to smell disposable.
Be frumpy or some petty despot in the form of a god
will abduct you to be its wine-pourer, page-turner,
on-call provider. Things could get worse.
You could be working in a veneer mill
choking on sawdust orange air, the rattiest head-to-knees
hundred-year-old homegirl, hauling wood on a sledge
while a mountain of pulp grows behind you.

 Would you rather be an ornament or a mule?
Loneliness is heavy lifting. Despair is heaven breaking.
To think is to be sick. And if I cried who'd hear me.

 Does your feeling congeal to a hard unspeakable?
Word. It's nothing just something = = night or life = =
installed a = = in my gift. Smiling won't hide it.

 Is it a mini-anvil maybe? No sweat.

 You will carry the day, door by door.

 Is it unexploded ordnance? No problem.

A small service mammal? Don't fret.
Shunn'd persons! I will be your poet.
I will love more to you than to any of the rest.
It's some kind of havoc canister.
It's some kind of primitive pump.

Hundred-Year-Old Homegirl

If I'd had a friend back then—traveler, pilgrim, shadow—
I'd have memorized her
ingénue perfumes: Ambush, Tigress, Cotillion, Woodhue—
till one evening at The Peerless
I'd win a door prize that ejaculated
a mist of fetching newness, Chanel N°22.
She'd starve along with me, this friend in this

long ago that must be reckoned in geologic time.
We'd splurge on Milky Ways, eat them all the way
home, giga-, mega-, kilo-years ago, gorging on sugar
as we rushed through the city's roughness
in our schoolgirl uniforms, having our asses grabbed
by boys who shamed us, showed us
how nothing females were, that no

bravado could save us. If I had a friend
she'd mix her liquor with me,
then hold my long hair back above the sink.
I'd admire her unladylikeness
when ladylike meant warping yourself
into what was seemly and convenient
for the world. There'd be no dissembling

about her, this friend who'd give me a mod ensemble
when she had precious little, who'd cry
for living things—turtles, fish—who can't cry
for themselves when damaged.
If I had a friend back then—traveler, pilgrim, shadow—
he'd throw a scarf over his bedside lamp
to cast a lubricated glow and rock

a motley shirt his grandmother sewed
from factory remnants. He'd quit his job in protest
when I got fired and get lost with me.
He'd work the wheel while I worked
the accelerator and brake. Collisions
create continents. Open the storm window.
Let him sing it into you, the storm.

If I had a friend—traveler, pilgrim, shadow—
he'd bake a mean chocolate chip, stitch me a skirt,
send letters that fed me.
He'd inscribe the unabridged
in a fluent hand that praised my hands.
His accent would romance the air.
Let that voice in, you. Listen well into the night.

If I saw one of these true ones coming,
carrying a kitten or guitar, a rapidograph pen,

60

every nerve in me would jump,
anointed with a giddy joy. One cross-dressed,
smoking a clove cigarette. One bounding
more than walking, trying to take off
with each stride. One who'd go the distance

on a Trailways to be my saving grace.
At my mother's funeral we'd sing "Let It Be"
in the vestibule when the priest refused to
let that song inside the church.
If I had a friend she'd listen
when teaching bled me out.
When I was a tree turned into timber,

a fate worse than Daphne's, tell me about it!
she'd exclaim. Traveler, pilgrim, shadow——she'd shout
with glee at my triumph and confide
that a double agent had betrayed me
to the Dean. O groans of academe.
Those days turn like pages in the Book of Kells,
prick marks and guidelines still visible.

If I had a——well, get a grip on lucky, you. On gifts.
She'd starve along with me, this friend in this
nothing females were for the world.
There'd be no dissembling. Cast a glow and rock.

Let him sing it into you, the storm.
Let those voices in, you. Listen well
into the night. Friends who'd go the distance

when you were a tree turned into timber,
prick marks and guidelines still visible.

Four

Snatch

A bee his burnished carnage. His battle bling of stripes.
Dove boldly in a Rose. Honey dunker.
To knit him fast to her—his goods.
Combinedly alighting—Himself—his Equipage.

She would not be the flower, bristling
with submission. She would be self-
sealing. The female portion at the center
is the pistil. Her Life had stood—a Loaded Gun—

A social insect, he spoke in pastoral
to the larger buzz he was abbreviation of:
The first thing to know about
your penis is it is not your penis.

It is God's penis. You are simply borrowing it.
While God's penis is on loan you must admit that
it is sort of just hanging out there
very lonely as if it needed a home. He gyrated

on the surface of the hive
to preach: *God created a woman to be your wife*
and when you look down you will notice that
your wife is shaped differently than you

and makes a very nice home. He gave
each guy two stones, saying
God is giving you your balls back
to do kingdom work. Put these on

your monitors or glue them
to your dash. Men flew in to attend.
The offering swelled. His burnished Carriage.
He is what he has. Sweet sacker.

The bride elect, the Rose—withholding knot
to his Cupidity. Their Moment. Mated.
Remains for him—to flee—
Remains for her—of capture—

Remastering strategies.

Plaster Cast Torso Of Apollo

We can infer his long-since looted head
with eyes like curated hail. And that his chest
is still benumbed by empire from above,
as if a morgue, in his glare, now canonized,

fires an arctic solstice. Otherwise, the pocked tits
could not oppress you, and Victory
would not grin through smug ligaments
to reach that sperm hive where priapism lived.

Otherwise, this bust would seem impugned
by the rude graffiti, **AR**T, that's spraybombed on it,
and would not slutshame like a frat boy's tweet:

would not, from every morsel of itself
extrude a tomb: for here there is no flesh
to witness for you. You must be those eyes.

Coloratura On An Apparatus With Star-Shaped Cells

"For the animals it is an eternal Treblinka."
—Isaac Bashevis Singer

The interviewer should be like light
          invisibly making things visible.
Should I sew my eyes closed?
          It was impossible to see it
and be undefiled.

          They needed out-
put from the soft side
          to draw a story.
That's where I came in.
          Should I make a heart

or a diamond
          of it? When witnessing it's best
to whip in sunshine blurts to soften
          trauma blobs. Treblinka,
what a pretty word!

          When publicizing experiment results do you consider rhetoric, style?
What better than a couple of classic kitten studies in the style of Todman! He was

not a man to merely decorate an office with his presence. His was the renowned study of kittens who could not visually adjust to a distorted environment without acting upon that environment. Cat brains might be tiny human brains, which makes them very useful.

How did you distort the environment?
We sewed their eyes closed.

Sleep gives distance, if you can reach it.
    If we could travel
to the birth of starlight,
    the star would disappear.
Sleep is like that. Go fast asleep, sleep quick
    because you cannot sleep
unvisited. Night is likeminded, riled,
    day a hyperbole of why.

Do sleepers know they're sleeping?
Funny you should ask! Knowing one aspect of a thing often precludes knowing others. Our Rat Study of Total Sleep Deprivation used constant light, a disk-over-water or flowerpot apparatus, recording devices implanted in the cortex, and intraperitoneally implanted radio transmitters to prove sleep, at least in the Rat, is a biological necessity.

Is it brilliant or is it stupid?
        Is he just talking
loosely as they must do in his in-
        clump in-
creasing their own insularity by ex-
        cluding the un-
defended out-
        clump? For I know the human
is a territorial animal
        ever ready to spray.
But that is not kind.
        I am speaking of the kind,
the kind that have the right.
        Is it just
tribal? Or do they do so
        because the world so
wills it?

        "The question is not, Can they reason? nor Can they talk? but,
        Can they suffer?" Asking for a friend.
That's a tough nut to crack! Rodents aren't covered by The Animal Welfare Act,
so we can operate on them without pain-killers. They're unpopular, so no exper-
iment on them is illegal, no anesthesia is needed. I can say we think of them with
affectionate gratitude. In fact, one Rat Man's classic book was dedicated to "Mus
norvegicus albinus," the white rat.

-ᴡᴡ|||ᴡᴡ-

When compassion is snuffed,
     the lack night begins.
Though we have not created it, we have not
     not created it.
Ignorance has its sour. Intelligence is ill.
     If you only == you will be accused.
No, we can't have that!
     If I thought God were listening
I'd say death takes place
     while we're alive
so why can't paradise?

     Can your experiments == imagine?
Can they ever! Imagine mice trained with foot shocks to fear the scent of cherry blossoms. Imagine glow-in-the-dark monkeys injected with virus-carrying jellyfish genes. In one wacky little stunt, the head and forelegs of a puppy were grafted to the neck of an adult dog whose heart pumped blood for both. Imagine! Though it had almost no body of its own, the puppy head playfully growled, licked the hand that caressed it, and eagerly lapped milk when its host was thirsty. At first the big dog looked confounded and tried to shake it off, but the pair lived over a month. They then were stuffed and toured for exhibitions.

There are techniques
     that harden kindness.
Euphemize. Miniaturize.

Turn a guillotine
into a toy or charm.
        Am I a filter, an intestine
torture passes through
        in different gravities
on its way to being
        tamed? Kindness gutted.
As if knowledge could ease suffering.

        Do you think the animals == mind?
That's a good question! We thought why not add some mind-like variable? So we
injected brain cells from donated human fetuses into Rat. And these human pro-
genitors colonized the entire brain. They became astrocytes, star-shaped cells.
The Rat cells fled to the margins. These humanized Rats remembered sounds
linked to electric shocks four times longer than the controls.

There are those who will say
        they are un-
like us. Though their use-
        fulness depends upon their being
almost i-
        dentical. I
speak to you who are.
        If you *only*.
Let witness in. Let empathy.

The heart pumps blood for both.
I'd like those who send the future
      to give when they are told
have a knowledge
      drawn by mercy.
And the voice of *only*
      will have a friend.

    After the tests what happened to Kitten, Rat, Mouse, Monkey, Dog?
They were sacrificed.
    Killed?
Cervical dislocation produced lethality.
    Death?
If still alive, they were injected with dissonance reduction.
    Killed?
It had that effect.

Should I make a heart
      or a diamond of them?
You can make a heart
      by drawing a half-circle in a corner.
A diamond is harder.
      I wanted to study
how folly was dissolved.
      So I made a brain.

An apparatus with star-shaped cells,
        a tiny brain becomes a toy.
I sewed mine closed
        on its way to being tamed,
injected sunshine blurts. Controls.
        For dissonance reduction
imagined == a listening paradise.
        Is it human or is it stupid? Do we know

we're sleeping? Colonized.
        The world so wills it.
You sewed your soul closed?
        It had that effect.
And the apparatus?
        The apparatus was too cold
to melt the edifice.
        This brain I made.

Intra-Articular Shaver Gift Box

Are you squeamish? he asked. A beige hard-body case cosseted the instrument. It was said to possess "exquisite structures." In an act of miraculous bench science, I was to assemble it in order to comprehend it. It could do remarkable things. Debride. I imagined its blades moving faster than a hummingbird's wings, faster than a master barber's scissors. I was working for this agency. Their only copy-writer, I was to decoct a thick slush of rough notes into crystalline instructions surgeons could peruse. Though I had no medical knowledge. Though I was deeply squeamish. I mostly wrote bloated slogans, direct mail blah-blah, snappy body copy, earcatching radio spots. *The Yankees are New York!* I flogged TV movies based on bodice rippers or Nazis, my ignorance no hindrance. I was a tool using language as a tool to create a crude desire.

The manufacturer's notes contained no color, though the body broken into would. As I was thinking this, a pickpocket on the rush hour bus lifted my wallet and charged $500 at Tie City. He'd hawk this neckwear in Times Square, near three-card-monte dealers and eternal going-out-of-business signs. "I Will Survive." After lavish agency dinners, I cried to Gloria's anthem in the traffic-strangled taxi while dancers hustled furiously at Studio 54, close to where I lived.

I imagined the instrument might sound like the ice cream man's truck from childhood, its freezer full of bluesky popsicles. Like razor blade wind chimes. At least there was no blood in the instructions. What had become of it? There was no sweat, tears, phlegm, synovial fluid. It was about the body being done to, not what the body could do. It could do remarkable things. Would you like a hot towel? Just finish me off with a dash of lilac. It was hand-crafted and had undergone the boiling water test. Its failure load had been hypothesized. It was storm colored and couldn't feel or think. That was its limitation. No, that was its gift.

Suffering Can Be Eased With Poppies

and pillows sprayed with lavender.
      Lavender demands an extravagance of sun.
Extravagance needs a single-drop waterfall,
a fiesta cup to caffeinate the day.
      The body's hidden fiesta is blood,
which requires a skin to live in.
      Poverty will live on
a yoga mat and bowl of rice
but prayer wants an enhancement
of candles to solve the planet's anguish.
      Cold easel syndrome needs solvents
to resuscitate the canvas.
      Sickness canvasses the world
for water mixed with gold dust
but fortune's rough justice won't suck up.
      Ozone's extra molecule
sucks the stench of frangipani
from a drippage of infinity
scarves while snow
sedates the wreckage of what-is.
      It will take a superflux
of snow to calm a world
this wired with overness.
      Sadness can be calmed

by aroma therapy, but grief can't
flush the fragrance from its mind.
      The mind is hushed
by mantras, but trauma has a tongue
so long it wraps around the inside of the skull.

Isadora's Scarf

It was the beginning of winter, of breathing
made visible, the air like shrapnel made steam.
I sat in his chair in my shiver
nightgown while he was dying. The prayers
I knew were mildewed
from darkness and disuse. Please, a mantra.

It wasn't fair == it wasn't fair

that we breathed. All my life he'd be with me
but he wouldn't be with him. It was November
and would always be. Thoughts stream back
like Isadora's scarf, snarling round a wheel.

The past is thrashing == the dust is ringing.

No, it is the phone. I race breakneck down the midnight ==
my sister says wake Mother == he's asking ==
but she'd arrive too late. To exist is to become this

instant == evanescent

as the line left by a skate. I'll be seeing you,
he'd say. Though I'd be seeing him.

After he died, he appeared by my bed,
trying to give me cash. When Ma, bereft,
said if only he were here to help, I turned = =

impatient = = snapping

didn't he do enough, and somehow comforted,
she repeated, even leaned on, my harsh words.
Keep the faith, she'd wave as I rushed

out the door. When she was dying
caregivers transfused her room with trance
music like auditory embalming grog. *Jesus!*

It was the first time I'd heard her cry to him
for help. And I wanted to recrucify
the Savior for not saving, not listening = =

it wasn't fair = = it wasn't fair
the past is thrashing = = the dust is ringing
instant = = evanescent
impatient = = snapping

I wanted to wrench the ear protectors
from the head of the Protector. But I had to
pry my hands away from my ears first.

Five

Air Voice

It might help to think we live in the head-
      waters, that infinity
comes in different sizes and its recombinant
      astonishment factor
can be seen as sky. That even the planet wobbles
      as it spins and water shakes
whatever it reflects. That we do suffering
      very well. Just keep shell
growth ahead of body size.
      Be sensitive to perpetuals
and don't try to train the rainbow
      to stack its colors differently.

Science says an error of one
      part in ten billion is good enough,
and physics is mostly about stuff
      bumping into each other.
Ice is your friend, the smart phone advised
      before breaking up into what
sounded like *bandaging your closure*
      and *there's a giant preen gland in your rump.*
We'll take up the special case of silence
      in good time.

When things get heavier
     on burning == when the smoke is weighed.

      ⎍⌣⧫⎍⌣⎍

Today we will make liquid nitrogen ice cream!
     the kindergarten teacher enthused.
Chacun à son goût. The woodland caribou
     lives on 150-year-old lichens and whatever
the great horned owl is saying must be said
     in B-flat. Rests are motion with zero speed,
the composer noted, and the phone heard
     death's an emotion where zero peed.
A mane carved of granite will validate the wind,
     the sculptor claimed. You'll be a ventifact,
a pebble shaped by me, said the breeze.
     You'll be gothic with reaching, said the tree.

      ⎍⌣⧫⎍⌣⎍

What's faster than light cannot be
     willed. It must flash by in a pirate way,
the physicist insisted. It must enter existence
     unpredictably and be the life of it.
The giver can't control the gift.
     If the directions say follow
the pink stripe after the green, just follow
     the clouds. Though using two maps

lets the heart of the matter fall
      through the cracks, the navigator warned.
Thoughtsarelockswithfrightbetweeneachflick.
      That was the password hint.

Things get heavier on yearning
      when the hope is weighed.
Try standing with a book on your head,
      groaned the caryatid.
Give me your passion and I'll burn in its honor,
      the candle offered as the giftshop said
this is not a building in distress,
      and the air voice rasped is there a heartbeat
in the house? It was paging all envisioners
      on the nightjar shift. Here they come
in their dun scrubs
      bearing their grave gifts.

Most And Great

She told them about the paper in her, an old kind
of printing plant or drawing room, a profusion
free with green on last year's growth, the past
an enthrallment larger than the present. Paper
lanterns, blue aerograms. They spoke of themselves
as most and great and lived the etymology of hand:
sidedness, possess. Though it was sweet
to stand with them with the wind drinking dawn,
she felt missed. Uneasy. Romance felt shot.
Paper had installed in her tears and love.
But everything decayed—fruit tree, yew,
even those stupid lawns she hated.
The dance floor fed up, grieving, the garden
always arguing that it should be called a park.

Wildest Word In The Language Advisory

The invitation arrived in the mist
and I didn't know how to say no.
I'd had no no practice and I was afraid
my no might be abrasive.
I needed a decorative negation.
      Just say I have to go pull my groceries home on a sleigh.
I needed a pillow word, a concept from Japanese poetics:
a phrase that is a set piece without much meaning,
which also happens in ancient Greek. The wine-dark sea.
      Say I have to go out into the fields of learning,
      I have to look into Chapman's Homer.
Pillow words are a form of silence. Time has gutted them.
They're linguistic fossils. Lace-trimmed yawns.
      Say I have to look for a word
      crappily adapted to my own catastrophe.
They're figures of speech that always cushion certain nouns.
      Say I have to consider why "autumn mountains"
      always modifies "moving colors."
Moving means touching, colors that can make you cry.
Ornament can be important.
      Say I have to think why *Mina no wata*,
      marsh snail guts, always modifies darkness.
As linguistic sizing, pillow words
are sometimes left untranslated.

Say I have to go untranslate some
pre-fabs, ready-mades. White noise.
Under the militant screws of too much meaning,
I have to whisper shh.
Originality can be draining. Please give it a rest.
Say I've reconsidered my wine-dark cognition project
and I'm going to fill my fill with cheap bubbly instead.
The way dweebish poser prats trying to be cool
spangle their language with *right?* a tic
that fishes for agreement but meets resistance
from listeners thinking *wrong*. Like *like*, a word used with abandon
where there's no comparison, like
you know, a phrase assuming comprehension where none exists.
Say I have to you know go feed my like peace foundry, right?
When you're heavy-headed, when you need to secede,
there is this rest ice. A cushion word
placed beneath a suffering
can comfort. Some contain little songs.
In the treetop. When the wind blows.
Say I have to go listen to ambient chill music.
It comes with lullaby instructions.
"Not fast, with tender expression."
The cradle will fall and—
darkness darkness, be my pillow.
Say I have to tie a white bow on the Coachman's whip.
Is that a soporific drink—like a white zombie?

Or the one who carries a coffin with him everywhere?
The one who looks liturgical. With jangling golden wings.
        Say I have to consider the radiance.
Habits develop a dynamism of their own, a centrifugal force,
and the edge where everything happens is undermined.
        Say I have to go listen to the pitter-patter
        of snowflakes in the Arctic desert.
I was in the *yes* habit, a word that locked me in the mist of this
barren rayon murmurous damask unbelustered slush.
Where I was nothing more than sullied colorwheel putty,
less and less. Because *yes* is docile, so tailwagging
a word. While *no* is a devouring host, the hex-
agonal blast of a stop sign in the rush.
        Just say I have to go theorize semiotic scroll notation,
        the emergence of maize culture film footage,
        and snorkel-aided computation.
        I have to go worship ground-figure reversals,
        find the camphorwood box
        where Millicent Todd Bingham stored Dickinson's papers,
        land a kissable tomboy sinecure
        and make nonnegotiable demands.
        But first I have to go pull my groceries home on a sleigh.
I have to research the word *no*. Its very existence troubles.
After I said it I felt the best I'd ever felt
while feeling bad. When I glanced out the window
the wind was asking. And the mist was answering.

Coloratura On A Dissonance Heard In Reticent Librettos

Because my brook is fluent,
I can sleep without a clock under my ear
     To imitate a true love's heart.
Lip to lip and rough and tumble,
its job is just to fondle rocks.

     Because I live where it lives
I don't need snapshots of lava
lamps to generate true randomness.
     I don't need the OED. Did you mean:
Because my *book* is fluent?

Some figures are not figurative, so predictable
     machine. Fluency disorders ==
cluttering, prolongations,
secondary escape behaviors ==
     are what its music's made of.

     -ww/Mww-

I did a year of reticence theory and learned
falling is noisier than flowing,
a waterfall is a stream changed to ovation,
silence is the voice of glacier blood,
the dark white that lives

between the lines. Rest ice.
The white bow on the Coachman's whip.
The velvet backing on the frame.
White noise is sonic silence.
That's why I did a dissertation on applause.

My survey encouraged all beholders
in their reckoning frames
to inspect ovations
at their leisure and confirm
in which part of which emotion
the praise conserved in
such collisions took place.

We studied those who clapped
with hands held high
so all could see them fawn,
and those who brooded,
sitting on their digits.

If you are silent about your pain, they'll kill you
and say you enjoyed it.
And they'll kill you if you speak up.
Unconsciousness begins with white noise,

a static roaring in the head.
Consider the stormborn applause for Stalin.
The first to stop will be shot!
If your hands burn afterwards,

it is militant quietude speaking.
Acclaim has such momentum.
There's a need for salvo stays.
At home in his dacha, Stalin had no carpets.

He wanted to hear the footsteps approaching.

·We are exhuming silence considered for this moment
        to be made of earth.
The preferred method requires a toothless backhoe
        followed by small scrapes
till hush fragments appear: *Because. my.*
        Next we need a crew to pedestal
the remains. *Brook. is. fluent.*
        To dig a trench, show the edges
and sieve the ground
        for bits: *I. know. 'tis. dry—*
A difference in compaction signals a disturbance
        decades past. *Because. my.* Check the icicles
for lineation. *Brook. is. silent.* Long buried

silence resembles rock shards with the power to cut
what's solid or dense. *It. is. the. Sea*——
        When only the largest quiet is exposed
and moved the project's called a symbolic lift.
        And. startled. at. It means the quiet is
figuratively in a new place but literally split.
        its. rising. It isn't pale like a cow bone
exposed. *I. try. to. flee.*
        It's dirt-colored and hard to identify.
To. where. You have to put your tongue
        to it. *the. Strong. assure. me.* Silence will stick
because it's porous. *Is. "no. more. Sea*——*"*
        The tongue will stick to hush.

-\ww\||\ww-

When truth is replaced by silence, silence is a lie.
We are studying
the ways that solitude cures loneliness.
Students, don't sit at such a distance.
I want to hear your minds groaning
as the trees do on a bitter night.
I read something corrosive in your reticence
that scares me stupid.
Though fluency seems glib
as a babblebrook in spring.

-\ww\||\ww-

When my brook is in its music,
I don't miss muppets belting out
      a power ballad, folksongs banged
on marrow bones with cleavers,
a wandering harp and fiddle.

      By August, it's almost dry
and gone to loss and still
I'm subject to its gift. Lovely
      its stuttering. Lovely its lilt.
Because I live where it lives

it has this giddiness effect
      on me. Its leathery pebble
of a frog and murk-colored
turtle in her pelt of mud
      can please me I'm so pleased.

-ww/WWww-

I have invented a new genre. That of silence.
Isaac Babel. O babblebook in spring.

When you cut the nice-nice
what oozes out?

Sugar foam, pastel curdle howls.
The ecopoet composing an eclogue

on global warming while
eating a hamburger.

-wwﾙﾙﾙﾙﾙﾙww-

I was meditating to the silence of a bell
at rest. After the carillon, this bell

kept sounding. This stilled bell
spoke to everything

around it there
being a constant frottage

between its metal
and the elements. It

resonated with ambient
sounds and made a constant

low tolling. There was a constant
tamboura between

the bell and say the garden,
a vibration vibration

sensors could amplify.
Because the bell

is always ringing.
Its repose is silence-like

but it is not
silence. It is

ringing. It is rung
by your by

any presence.

A chirpy bird, a carpenter bee,
the roofers' hammering, the gruffness
of the mower, the mild
crash of crockery and cupboards closing,
a droning jet, the scrape of mouse
and crepitus of keyboard clicks—

Why would silence exist?

There is nothing
in the nature of
things that requires it.

He always made an awkward bow.

The silence at the end

should be heard

as the sound of held applause.

Reticence must respect the limits of its user.
Begin with a typical brute
algorithm that lists, categorizes, ticks off,
eliminates, then represses predilections.
Try the procedures by which ordinary people go about
being modestly rational. Are you a leaper or a plodder?
Do you thirst for redundancy or newness?
If the choice yields the full latitude of a radiant instance

you have it made. There's something
about a closed universe where your quietude is
waiting. That's what I was given
to believe. Change the soul and see
how strategies change to meet it. Then change the rain.
Nobody, not even the truth, has such slant hands.
Please slap me if I get too Zen.
Sir, they said, Ma'am, your silence is waiting for you.
To be praised by it was to be tasered by honey.

Six

Once Or Ever Let Alone Again Enthronement

Of snowflakes I can say
        I admire their courteous way of falling,
the calm with which they espouse their claim
        followed by a silent compounding.
Falling should be noisy.
        Their quietism seems a violation
of the convivial.
        Does each differentiate itself
from others through negotiation?
        No. No crystal would insist
it is the one
        all others should be modeled on.
Everyone knows it's possible
        to gather an infinitude
and not find two alike.
        But that is just a hypothesis
that's been hammered into fact.

        Of you I can say
the likelihood of anybody anything
        like you falling into being
once or ever
        let alone again is nil.

Yet you don't differentiate yourself
        by boasting or insist
you are the one
        all others need to be.
Nothing about you is compulsory.
        There are few useful heavenly bodies
relative to where I am.
        Though mortal,
you are a way to feel
        the presence of a presence
belonging more to wish
        than to existence existing.

A Token On June 9th

A flashmob of violinists playing Mozart is a marvel
because they won't play forever. Imagine if they did.
Forever is more frightening than *ephemeral*.
But nothing frightens time. If you listen you'll overhear
       the heartbeat of the doomsday clock. Say what?
       Overhear means hear too much.
       When it comes to time, the give must come
       from us. There are techniques
that soften thingness. In solidarity,
my preferred pronoun is *it*. If justice bathed the planet
would the infusion expand the confiscated past?
Ask forensic architects studying tear gas.
       I study tears. The exposition is as simple as possible
       and no simpler. Free body diagrams from the overhead
       projector contain more arrows than St. Sebastian,
       but my subjects are disfigured by love.
If you move the experiment you must move
everything relevant. When everything relevant

might be the entire cosmos how lucky
for me every relevance is you. Absolute time,
       math time, isn't cowed or bullied by anything
       external. But that's not how time works for us.
       You appeared like a book falling open

at a fortunate page. By chance
I was much favored. Now I'm afraid
you'll be taken in much the same way.
I wish my abrasions and mistakes could melt
like the wax tablets of antiquity
  into a forgiveness. Miracle.
  Ask the nun who thinks relics
  can manifest, whirr
  from nothingness to substance. It is true
every day in some metabolism
not necessarily but possibly this one
orogeny redreams
the clock and mountains begin again.

Toys Turned On A Lathe

Here in the north of north
everything was formed by what ice did
to the land, and darkness is redundant.
Night fills each mullion,
pressing itself into each
corner of each pane.
Like time it is everywhere
and has no edges. I sense
there's something large
that doesn't love us well.
Is it officious as a chancellor? It is
an omniscience = = a big think
piece that must I think consort
with wickedness.
But I am not its invigilator.

If I dim the inside, night will thin
and let me glimpse the quaking
forms outside. I find you
must create a likeness of
the dark for dark
to disappear. It requires a certain obeisance?
If it senses kinship it will yield = =
though only the spinning

iron crystal at earth's core
could be more noir. There is a power
at large that doesn't love us well.
It has a knowledge,
though I am not its proctor.

Everything here was formed by what ice did
to the mind. This is dark thinking.
Light might think
there's so much try to you. Stop crying.
In this interglacial moment,
you're in good flesh. Nox is nothing
but a sealed ark of ornaments.
When day breaks full of details
safe as toys turned on a lathe,
light predicts the innocent
will have a constellation named for them
as they any minute should.
There is darkness still behind the dark.
There is darkness. Still behind the dark
there might be shining on all sides.

Orogeny Compline

Muckland tanglewaters
wilderness that is
wild church with waves
like rocks come to life
& fathoms teal to bruise

I believe your shallow passages
are more dangerous than your deep

      that this terrain was shaped by ice
      & each tree hosts its own species of lichen
      while forests thrive
      on fire & pinecones
      use it to release their seeds

I believe in spring
the boreal forest frogs
will thaw from inside out
heart == brain == liver == limbs

      as the city flickers on the hill like vigil
      lights burning for the prayers
      they're burdened with
      I feel home

is an emotion ==
that meltwater led to mountains
made of remnants
between the lines == orogeny

that history lives in the dash
between two dates
& we can be here when it happens
underlaid with rift
& punctuated with granite

at this level of happy
in this holocene age okay

with contradiction lifted
into sunlight part of
the time & shaded at others

Psychopomps Are The Seraphs Who Carry Us

Think of the heavy lifting,
how they have their hands full
with their torches and keys. It can't be easy
to coax the soul away from every acquisition.

They must understand

the tenacity of the tiny grommets
that keep us here. Fitness machines
like humongous insects, internet
apparel sites. On one called Psychopomp
sullen goth models
flog a cryptic product—

t-shirts steeped in gnostic blessings.
It can't be easy
to wed the soul to its fate.
The change is vertiginous, the crossroads—
at Highways 49 and 61 in Clarksdale, Mississippi—
a gridlock of pilgrims on their knees.
Just try saying Phantom, tote me
into unknowing. I know
I'm not saying that. Here where there

is science and gravity,
each identical weight, when lifted,

will seem heavier than the one before.
It's a flaw in magnitude estimation

caused by time. But soul guides aren't indentured
to the temporal. They arrive from an age without age
and exist where time congeals.
They might travel with an animal—
a golden wolf or mountain pleasure horse,

their conveyance might be coach
and four or snowmobile.
They might be made of moon
rocks but their dusk
tunic and ankles inked with agape

testify to tactile contact with whatever
follows what-is. In classical depictions
they wear robes stitched from Carrara

yet their form extends indefinitely
and can't be frozen into stone.
Their scent—it has, I think, a hint of boreal forest—

exists only when a threshold
lawed by nature has been crossed.

They're impressive at all hours but never more
than midnight, the hinge between.
Keep a lamp—fluorescent diode gas or diesel
tungsten butter or nightingale—by the door

though grief best captures their features.

Icebreaker Escort, if you must come
while I'm drafting this, be patient.
The wind rose I'm constructing
indicates gale strength
by the thickness of the lines
that reach in 16 cardinal directions.

The circle in the center
shows degrees of calm. Here winds were calm
zero percent of the time. Soul Guide, help us
fasten our masks to guard against the fumes
of days on end. Remember your job
is not to judge or sentence. Please
lift us gently and give us time

to pack a few regrets.
If we miss the midnight trip

we'll catch the next.

Summoning A Freshening

Firstness, be merciful
to animals raised in the dark.
Time's minions. As I am.

Time's chattel. Lumpen.
As a bullet travels faster than its sound,
let compassion travel.

Though hierarchy be hardwired, dismantle it.
Undo otherness. I pray you.
And by praying you, I create you.

⌇

Let the next be restful.
After major sparkling, matte.

Let art spin a likeness for loneliness.
Let it be company. With stuff in it.
Let it wreck the wrecking ball.

Unleash the living
from my daunted head.

⌇

As color is sifted through a prism ==
soul is strained through world.

The quality of mercy falls
like small-caliber raindrops
on the place below: the slaughter-
house between the farm-to-table.
The classic kitten studies.

Time == was it == mind == was it ==
marbled me with knowledge.
Not like a steak that's tragic flesh.
More embossed endpaper.

Because knowing without going
through the suffering you know
is a mortal form of ornament,
the lace of shape.

-ᴠᴡ�ᴡ-

Sidereal force, bestow mercy
on the innocent. Nudge compassion
please toward them.
As plates under an ocean can
shove continents, vast array, you can.

-ᴠᴡ�ᴡ-

Just past midnight, December 31st,
I'm waiting for the other ball to drop.

But everything happens only once
when time's the boss.

The difference between time and music
is music can repeat. Dissonance seizes

our attention: doors slamming, earth moving
machines. As it pleases time

to wipe clean everything
we've touched,

of the inexpressible one
cannot say too much.

∿∿∿

I ask for absolution though I am as-is:
damaged, has-been, dissed. I was

guided by duty in the great things
and the small. There was this self-

flagellating map, this grind
of a cartographer being

flogged inside my head.
I traveled by diligence.

Grant me my walking papers.
As long as I'm alive

I'll institute myself and give
thanks each time I rise.

‑ᴡᴧᴡ‑

I don't ask for trophy travel.
Alarums and excursions
tire me. Sailing to Byzantium
in search of spicier jewels I might fail
to see my present wealth.
When explorers searching for Cathay
chanced on North America
            they tried to bribe or slash
a passage through or navigate around it,
thinking it an obstacle, not thinking
how immense == how home it was
            to others there before.
            Before that thought

takes flight let me be on it.
      Though I am tardy,
      ailing, affronted, raw,
let me recognize = = not colonize = =
the gift that bright exults me now.

Notes

"Coloratura On A Darkness Chosen From A Gamut Of Stygian Events" briefly riffs on a line from Walt Whitman's "Native Moments."

"Salt Point Vesper" quotes *The Education of Henry Adams* and alludes to a phrase from William Wordsworth's *Prelude, Book III.*

"A Thing Long Thought And Kind" recalls a line from "Roses Only" by Marianne Moore.

"One Toe Pointing Backwards Prodrome" contains an italicized line from William Wordsworth's *Prelude, Book I.*

"Blue Funk Stew Dialogic" quotes and reinscribes lines from "Native Moments" by Walt Whitman. A portion of the first line of "The First Elegy" of Rainer Maria Rilke's *Duino Elegies* also appears.

"Snatch" repurposes and quotes Emily Dickinson's poems #1351 and #764 (*The Poems of Emily Dickinson*, ed. R. W. Franklin, 3 vols. Cambridge, MA: Harvard University Press, 1998). The italicized lines were posted by Pastor Mark Driscoll (writing as William Wallace II) on a Mars Hill Church (Seattle) message board in 2001.

"Plaster Cast Torso Of Apollo" recasts Rainer Maria Rilke's "Archaic Torso of Apollo."

The epigraph for "Coloratura On An Apparatus With Star-Shaped Cells" is from "The Letter Writer" by Isaac Bashevis Singer. The quotation beginning "The Question is not, Can they reason?" is from Jeremy Bentham's *An Introduction to the Principles of Morals and Legislation*. Among many other sources, the sequence was informed by Hubel and Wiesel's classic kitten studies; Bergmann and Rechtschaffen's work on sleep deprivation in the rat; Dias and Ressler's research on the olfactory memories of mice; Sasaki, Suemizu, and Shimada's transgenic experiments with non-human primates; Vladimir Demikhov's two-headed dog operations; and Steven A. Goldman's chimeric rodent brain transplants.

"Wildest Word In The Language Advisory" remembers phrases from "Fields of Learning" by Josephine Miles; "Darkness, Darkness" by Jesse Colin Young; and "The City Limits" by A. R. Ammons.

"Coloratura On A Dissonance Heard In Reticent Librettos": Italicized lines are quoted from Zora Neale Hurston, Emily Dickinson, Yevgeny Yevtushenko, and Isaac Babel. The fifth section recalls a thought from *The Complete Prose of Marianne Moore*. A line in the last section rings changes on a line by e. e. cummings.

Acknowledgments

Blackbox Manifold: "Summoning A Freshening" with a few small differences. "Wildest Word In The Language Advisory" under a different title. "Coloratura On A Dissonance Heard In Reticent Librettos" with a different title and without the parts beginning "Because my brook is fluent" and "When my brook is in its music." Those inclusions are from "A Gift Economy," a poem published in the *Kenyon Review*.

Great Lakes: Image & Word. Allendale, MI: Grand Valley State University, 2016. Exhibition catalog. An earlier version of "Orogeny Compline" appeared under the title "Vessel" and was incorporated into the sculpture *Basin* by Kim Cridler.

Poetry: "Plaster Cast Torso Of Apollo."

Poets.org: "A Thing Long Thought And Kind" under a slightly different title.